FALLING INTO SIN

The story of the fall from grace and
of God's promise of a Savior, from
Genesis 2:15–25; 3:1–19, for children

Written by Martha Streufert Jander
Illustrated by Michelle Dorenkamp Repa

CONCORDIA PUBLISHING HOUSE • SAINT LOUIS

When God first created the world,
He made a man and his wife.
In His image He formed them,
Breathed His very breath into them.
He gave them the breath of life.

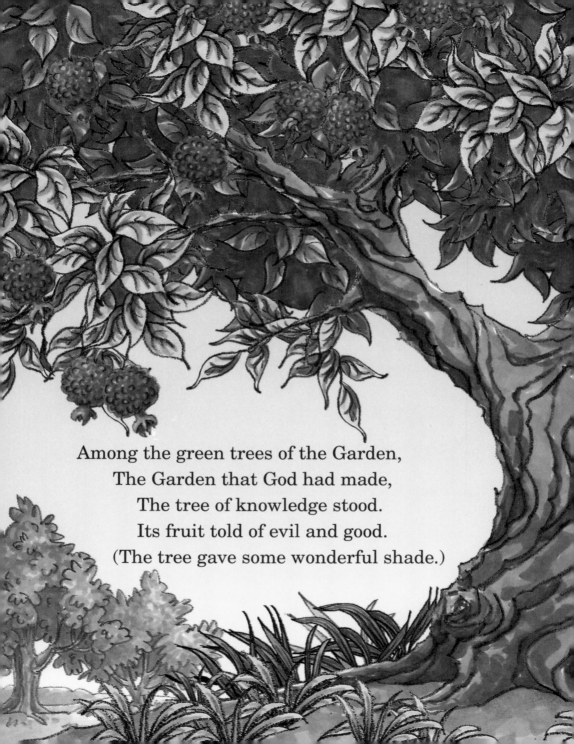

Among the green trees of the Garden,
The Garden that God had made,
The tree of knowledge stood.
Its fruit told of evil and good.
(The tree gave some wonderful shade.)

God gave Adam and Eve His instructions.
"With this law you must comply.
Of this fruit you must never eat,
The fruit of this one certain tree,
Or you will most surely die."

Now there was a snake in the Garden,
Who was the craftiest snake of all.
He made himself known to Eve—
The first one he planned to deceive.
He wanted them both to fall.

He asked Eve, "Did God indeed tell you
'You shall not eat of that tree'?"
Eve said, "God did say this,
Not to eat or even touch it.
If we do, we'll die—you'll see."

The serpent then lied to the woman,
"Look at the fruit of this tree.
You won't die," said the devil.
"You'll know good and evil;
Just like God, you soon will be."

Eve gazed at the fruit, so lush and fair.
It looked pleasant in her sight.
Longing just like God to be,
Grabbing fruit right off the tree,
She ate. Then Adam took a bite.

Adam and Eve, their eyes opened wide,
Knew for sure what they had done.
They had sinned—then came the shame.
Fig leaves were the clothes for them.
And they just wanted to run.

Then they heard God walk in the Garden.
They hid by bushes and trees.
Suddenly, they were afraid
Because they had disobeyed,
When before they'd been at ease.

"Oh Adam, where are you?" God called out.
Adam said, "I grew afraid
When I heard Your voice speaking.
I knew You were seeking."
God asked, "Have you disobeyed?"

God knew already that they had sinned;
He knew their fear and their shame.
Adam blamed it on Eve.
She said the snake deceived.
On the snake, she put all the blame.

God turned to the serpent and spoke a curse,
"On your belly now you'll crawl.
But one day I'll send a Savior
To save people forever.
And you are the enemy of all."

Yet God loved them. He spoke first to Eve,
"You'll labor when you have children.
Adam, you will work with strife.
You both will sorrow all your life,
But then you will go to heaven."

Dear Parent,

When Adam and Eve ate of the tree of the knowledge of good and of evil, they brought sin into the world. With sin came death and every kind of evil. This was not God's plan for His beautiful world. His plan had included a loving relationship with all He had made—especially with the crown of His creation, the man and woman into whom He had breathed His own breath.

Sin and shame bowed down the heads of our first parents. They did not become like God—as Satan had promised—but they did know good and evil. And God, in His great mercy and love, did not abandon them. In the words of Genesis 3:15, He promised to send a Savior. And He did!

After centuries, and in His time, God sent the Savior in the person of Jesus, His only Son. Jesus was born, lived, died, and rose again so that we might have a loving relationship with God, who forgives us for the sake of His Son and will one day indeed take us to heaven to live with Him forever.

When you read this book with your child, review the Christmas and Easter stories as a way to help your child understand how God reveals His plan for all people in the words of the Scriptures.

The author